21st Century

ism

Das

First published in 2005 by Wayland
© Wayland 2005
Wayland, 338 Euston Road, London NW1 3BH
This paperback edition published in 2009

Subject consultant: Dr Nick Sutton, The Oxford Centre for
Hindu Studies
Project Editor, Hodder Wayland: Kirsty Hamilton
Editor: Nicola Barber
Designer: Janet McCallum
Picture Researcher: Shelley Noronha, Glass Onion Pictures
Maps and artwork: Peter Bull

British Library Cataloguing in Publication Data
Rasamandala Das
21st century Hinduism. – (21st century religions)
1. Hinduism – Juvenile literature
I. Title II. Twenty-first century Hinduism III. Hinduism
294.5

ISBN 978 0 7502 5632 2

Colour Reproduction by Dot Gradations Ltd, UK
Printed in China

Wayland is a division of Hachette Children's Books,
an Hachette Livre UK Company.
www.hachettelivre.co.uk

The publisher would like to thank the following for permission to
reproduce their pictures: Alamy/Saulius T. Kondrotas 10; The
Bhaktivedanta Book Trust International. Copyright 2005. Used
with permission 13; Bhaktivedanta Manor 45; CIRCA Photo
Library/Bipin J. Mistry 4, John Smith 18, Bipin J. Mistry 23,
Bipin J. Mistry 24, John Smith 27, Bipin J. Mistry 29;
Corbis/Lindsay Hebberd 32; Eye Ubiquitous 41; Friends of
Vrindavan 44; Robert Harding Picture Library A. Tovy 11, A. Tovy
14, J.H.C. Wilson 22, J. Sweeney 30, A. Tovy 34, S. Grandadam
36; Hare Krishna Food for Life 42; Impact Photos 40; ISKCON
Educational Services 21, 43; Ann and Bury Peerless 7, 9, 16, 17,
20, 25, 33; Photofusion 39; Rex Pictures Ltd/Jeremy Hunter 31;
Topfoto 15, 19, 35, 38; ZUL 28

Contents

Note

In the Western world years are numbered as either BC ('Before Christ') or AD (Anno Domini – which is Latin for 'In the year of our Lord...'). In this book, the more neutral terms BCE ('Before the Common Era') and CE ('Common Era') are used.

Introduction

Hinduism is perhaps the oldest living religion in the world. It is difficult to say with certainty how it started. Unlike most other religions, it has no single founder, no one scripture, and no commonly agreed set of teachings. Throughout its long history, there have been many important religious leaders, teaching different philosophies and writing many holy books. For this reason, scholars often refer to Hinduism as 'a family of religions' or 'a way of life'.

Sanatan Dharma

Hinduism is at least four thousand years old. Many Hindus prefer to call their tradition *Sanatan Dharma*, meaning 'the eternal religion'. This name suggests a religion that it is timeless, teaching truths (such as the existence of the eternal soul) relevant to all people, at all times. Consequently, most Hindus do not reject other religions, believing them to be different paths towards the common goal of linking the soul with God. Hinduism is certainly closely connected with other 'eastern traditions' such as Jainism, Sikhism and Buddhism.

The Vedas

It is hard for everyone to agree on what is meant by Hinduism. Many Hindus say it refers to practices based on the teachings of certain holy books. These are the *Vedas* and their supplements (books based on the *Vedas*). 'Veda' is a Sanskrit word meaning 'knowledge'. This ancient wisdom was first passed down orally (by speaking) and only later written down (see page 7). Many scholars believe that the first book, the *Rig Veda*, was compiled between 1500 and 1000BCE, but was written down around 400BCE.

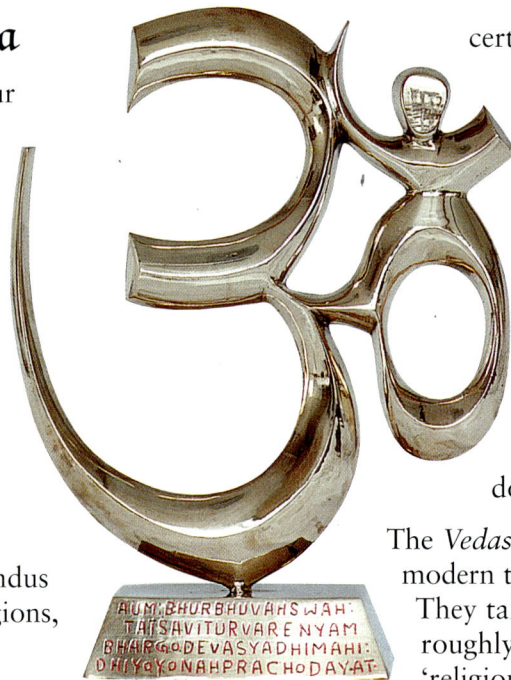

The *Vedas* themselves do not mention the modern terms 'Hindu' and 'Hinduism'. They talk about *dharma*, which roughly translates as 'religious law' or 'religious duty' (see page 14 for a full explanation of this term).

▲ The sign 'Om' is often used as the symbol of Hinduism. It is believed to represent the sound of creation. Hinduism teaches about the idea of successive creations, believing there is no absolute beginning or end to time. For this reason, Hindus often prefer to call their tradition Sanatan Dharma (the eternal religion).

► This map shows where Hindus live in the world today and places in India mentioned in the text.

The Hindu tradition

It is clear that what we now call 'Hinduism' has its roots in ancient India. Some scholars say the religion was brought into India by a group of people, known as Aryans, who invaded from Central Asia in about 1500BCE. Many Hindus dispute this, claiming that the Hindu tradition grew up in India itself, well before this time. The Hindu tradition often differs with Western ideas of time and evolution, claiming that human history, and its own heritage, go back indefinitely to previous glorious ages (see page 6).

Although Hinduism is complicated, there are three main strands:

1 *Vaishnavas* – who worship Vishnu (or his forms such as Rama and Krishna)

2 *Shaivas* – who worship Shiva (see page 15)

3 *Shaktas* – who worship Shakti, the goddess (usually in her form as Shiva's wife; see page 16).

In practice, many Hindus don't officially follow any of these strands – nor do they restrict themselves to just one. They often worship a number of deities. For this reason, and its general acceptance of other religions, Hinduism is known for being inclusive and tolerant. It is also misunderstood as being polytheistic (believing in many gods); in fact most Hindus believe in one Supreme God.

Hinduism worldwide

Although Hinduism is connected to India, its traditions and practices have now spread throughout the world. Major migration began in the 19th century, when Hindus went to live in places such as Fiji, Mauritius, the Caribbean, and South and East Africa. Many more moved in the late 1960s and early 1970s. There are now large communities of Hindus worldwide, especially in Europe and North America. India itself has many religions, but today over 80 per cent of its people follow the Hindu tradition.

Estimated number of Hindus (millions)

Over 500

1 - 25

up to 1

ॐ History and development of Hinduism

For a number of reasons, Hinduism's early history is complex and the subject of many theories. First, there are major differences of opinion between Hindus and Western researchers. Secondly, Hinduism is not a single religion, but includes many different branches. Thirdly, Hinduism has no definite starting point. It goes back at least four thousand years, and maybe much further. To study Hinduism thoroughly, it is important to understand its own world view.

The roots of the tradition

Hindus believe that time is eternal and that it moves in cycles of four ages (*yugas*), much like the four seasons. Apparently, during the first age – called the golden age – people were kind and religious. We now live in the fourth age – the iron age – typified by cruelty and materialism. Hindu people therefore question the idea that humans are always progressing. They also believe that genuine religion is eternal (Sanatan Dharma) and universal. It is not limited to one time, one country or any particular group of people.

Many scholars believe that Hinduism originated largely outside India. The Aryan invasion theory suggests that the Aryans conquered the Indus valley (in present-day Pakistan) around 1500BCE. The Aryans worshipped many deities connected with nature, especially Indra, the god of rain. They also brought with them the Sanskrit language, which has links to many European languages. Sanskrit is the origin of Hindi, the dominant Indian language today, and remains the language of Hindu prayer and study. The Aryans may also have brought their own social system with its different classes or *varnas* (see pages 14 and 37). Their own beliefs and practices may have mixed with those of the local Indus peoples, giving rise to what we now call Hinduism.

▼ *This diagram shows how the wheel of time rolls along in endless cycles of four ages. We are now just after the start of the fourth, shortest age, the age of iron. After this begins the next golden age.*

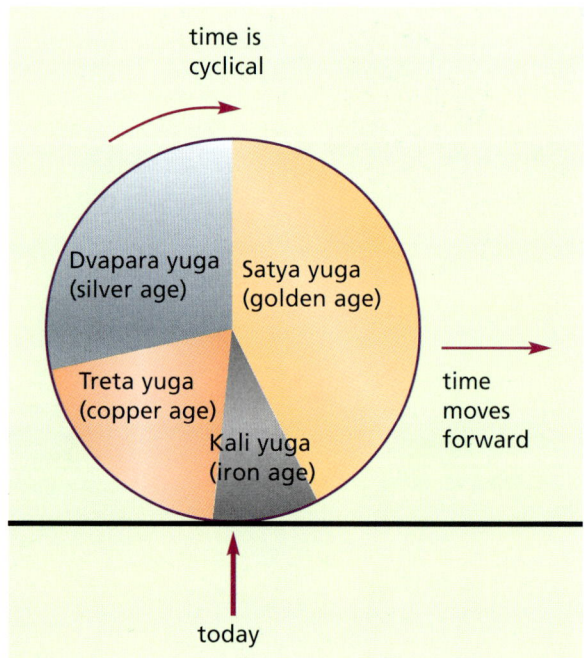

time is cyclical

Dvapara yuga (silver age)

Satya yuga (golden age)

Treta yuga (copper age)

Kali yuga (iron age)

time moves forward

today

The books are written

The teachings of Hinduism, initially passed down orally, were later written down. Tradition states that a sage called Vyasa recorded them on palm leaves about five thousand years ago, at the beginning of this age, the *Kali* yuga. Western scholars say that the first books, the *Vedas*, were composed later, from about 1000BCE onwards. During this period, the most common religious practice was the sacred fire ceremony, performed in honour of nature deities such as Indra, god of rain, and Agni, god of fire.

Later, the *Puranas* were composed, containing many of the stories still popular today. Scholars believe that most were written down between 500BCE and 500CE. During this period the fire ceremony was superceded by *puja* – the ritual worship of sacred images. Indra and Agni were no longer the main deities, but were largely replaced by Vishnu, Shiva and Shakti (also called Devi, the goddess). Two religions related to Hinduism, Buddhism and Jainism, also flourished during this time.

Poets and theologians

From about 500CE onwards, important thinkers laid the foundations for modern Hinduism. In the south of India, saints wrote hundreds of devotional poems, still recited in temples today. Amongst these saints was a woman called Andal, who continues to be venerated in southern India.

Later, beginning around 800CE, scholars, such as Shankara and Ramanuja, wrote detailed explanations of the sacred texts. They also developed their own specific doctrines, each passed down by an unbroken chain of *gurus* (teachers) and their disciples, known as a *sampradaya*. During this period, these thinkers developed two main ideas:

1 God is everywhere (and is everything)

2 God is also a person (beyond the world)

▼ Excavations at the ancient Indus valley city of Mohenjo-daro, now in modern Pakistan. Scholars say that archaeological and other evidence from such sites suggests that northwest India was invaded by the Aryans, who brought with them the beginnings of Hinduism.

The Mughal period

From the 8th century onwards, the new religion of Islam reached India via traders plying the Arabian Sea, and by the Muslim armies that conquered the northwest province of Sind. Muslim political power in India began with the Turks around 1200ᴄᴇ and culminated in the Mughal Empire which ruled India from 1526. The most famous Mughal emperor, Akbar (1542-1605), was extremely liberal and broad-minded and allowed Hindus to practise their faith freely. However, his great grandson, Aurangzeb, was ruthless, destroying temples and restricting Hindus in their practices. During the Mughal period, Hindus were somewhat excluded from public life.

The British Period

A British victory at the Battle of Plassey in 1757 heralded the end of the Mughal Empire and the rise of British supremacy in India. At first, the British did not interfere with the religion and culture of the Indian people, allowing Hindus to practise their religion with little outside influence. Later, however, missionaries arrived, determined to bring Christianity and their own versions of civilization to India.

The Reform Movements

In response, there arose a number of Hindu reform movements. Hindu thinkers became influenced by Western thought and while some adopted Western philosophical ideas and aspects of Christianity, others opposed them. In 1828, Rama Mohan Roy established the Brahmo Sabha incorporating ideas from both Christianity and from 17th- and 18th-century philosophers such as John Locke and David Hume. Other groups, such as the Arya Samaj, were concerned by attempts to convert Indians to Christianity. They tried to protect Hinduism, and simultaneously to free it from what they saw as its superstitious aspects, such as the worship of the *murti* (sacred image).

One of the most successful movements, establishing centres worldwide, was the Ramakrishna mission. It was founded in 1897 by the monk Vivekananda, who named it after his own spiritual teacher, Ramakrishna. Vivekananda impressed the Western world with his presentation on Hinduism to the World Parliament of Religions, at Chicago in 1893. He won a standing ovation by addressing the audience as 'Sisters and Brothers of America'. He subsequently presented a vision of religion that was inclusive and universal, based on the Hindu idea of the soul within all species of life.

The bhakti saints

The restraints of the Mughal era were made worse by the tight control kept by Hindu priests. Many of these brahmins, *members of the highest class, insisted on compliance with the hereditary caste system, which didn't permit Hindus of lower birth to take significant roles in society, or to advance in spiritual life. As a result, ordinary Hindus felt oppressed and leaders rose from amongst the people. These saints, known as the* bhakti *saints, emphasized the spiritual equality of everyone, and the need for personal morality and a mood of service. They expressed their religious feelings through song, music and poetry. A wave of devotion (bhakti) swept across India between 1400 and 1700.*

A poem by Mirabai

'We do not get a human life
Simply by asking.
Birth as a human
Is the reward for good deeds
In former births.
Life waxes and wanes imperceptibly,
And stays not long.
The leaf that has fallen
Returns not to the branch.
Behold the Sea of Reincarnation
With its swift, irresistible tide!
O Krishna, O pilot of my soul,
Swiftly conduct my ship to the other
    shore.
Mira, the servant of Krishna, declares,
"Life lasts for but a few days only."'

Mirabai was one of the main bhakti saints, and her poems are still popular today. They speak of her tireless devotion to Lord Krishna, one of the main Hindu deities. They also refer to other important Hindu ideas, such as karma, reincarnation and moksha or liberation (see page 13).

◄ Swami Vivekananda. His teachings grew out of the growing contact between India and the West. Other reformers promoted a different type of Hinduism, connected with nationalism and a strong sense of Indian identity. Most important was Mahatma Gandhi (see page 38) who opposed British domination of India and the depletion of the country's immense wealth. He was instrumental in India's gaining independence.

9

Independent India

The partition (division) of India in 1947 into two separate countries – Pakistan and India – was accompanied by considerable violence. Large numbers of Muslims headed for the newly created, and predominantly Muslim, Pakistan. Many Hindus and Sikhs fled in the opposite direction, seeking refuge within the newly drawn boundaries of India. There were bloody clashes between the two streams of refugees – between communities that had previously lived together in relative harmony. These upheavals reinforced the emerging ideas of India being a Hindu country, and of Hinduism being an Indian religion.

Hinduism goes global

In the 1960s many Hindus began to migrate to the West, especially to Britain and the USA. At the same time, many Hindu gurus (religious teachers) travelled to the West.

They helped to support the growing Hindu communities and started missionary movements that attracted Western interest. Many Westerners began to practise meditation and *hatha-yoga*, a form of exercise that nurtures inner peace (see page 25).

In the late 1960s, the Transcendental Meditation organization became popular throughout the world, and its spiritual leader, Maharishi Mahesh Yogi, attracted the attention of celebrities such as the Beatles. One of the most conspicuous groups at the time was the Hare Krishna movement, whose male followers shaved their heads and wore traditional saffron-coloured robes.

▼ *Members of the Hare Krishna Movement in the USA. Although termed a 'new religious movement', the organization goes back to Chaitanya, one of the bhakti saints. Its members became famous worldwide for their chanting and dancing in the streets of towns and cities.*

Modern Hinduism

During the late part of the 20th century, Hindu groups and communities became well-established throughout the developed world. Far and wide, in North America, Britain, South Africa and Australia, Hindu people flourished socially, academically and economically. At the hearts of their communities, they built expensive and impressive new temples.

In India itself, religious unrest continued. In 1984, tensions between the Hindu and Sikh communities came to a head when government forces stormed the Sikh headquarters, the Golden Temple in Amritsar. The subsequent assassination of Prime Minister Indira Gandhi, apparently by her Sikh bodyguards, further strained relationships between the previously close communities. Violence between Hindus and Muslims continued too, for example in the late 1990s, when there were angry clashes over the mosque built at Ayodhya (the birthplace of Rama, an important Hindu deity; see page 19). There was also continuing controversy over apparent attempts to convert Hindus to other religions, such as Christianity and Buddhism.

These historical trends have prompted modern Hindus to try to redefine their tradition, often as a separate religion. Despite these changes, the ancient tradition continues to flourish, primarily as a path towards spiritual and social well-being. Hinduism now extends well beyond India, nurtured by a number of well-organized movements with followers throughout the world.

▼ *The Swami Narayana Temple in London was opened in 1995. It is built of marble in a traditional Indian style of architecture. The Swami Narayana Mission has temples worldwide, and is headed by a well-known guru called Pramukh Swami.*

2 Hindu teachings and holy books

Hindus do not place much importance on everyone believing the same thing. They stress more the need for sincere spiritual practice, and the courage for humans to sometimes change their minds. Despite this flexible approach towards belief, there are some ideas shared by practically all Hindus. These include the *atman* (soul), reincarnation, karma and moksha (liberation). However, although belief in God is widely accepted, there are many different opinions about his nature and identity.

Atman – the eternal soul

Hindus believe that the atman is the 'real self' or the 'soul'. It is eternal and made of *brahman* (spirit). The mind and the body are made of matter.

In the religious text the *Bhagavad Gita* (see page 20), Krishna (one of the forms of Vishnu) explained how all of us experience that the body is changing at every moment.

Spirit and matter

Spirit (brahman)	Matter
Never-changing	Ever-changing
Eternal	Temporary
Conscious	Unconscious
Dynamic	Inert

'Those who are seers of the truth have concluded that matter (the body) is always changing and that spirit (the real self) never changes. This they have concluded by studying the nature of both.'

(Bhagavad Gita 2.16)

However, we – the atman (the real self within the body) – remain the same throughout our lives, despite changes to the mind and body. Krishna compared the body to a vehicle and the soul to the driver. He also compared the body to clothes which eventually wear out and therefore need replacing.

Reincarnation

Hindus believe that the atman, or soul, leaves the body at the time of death. It is carried in the astral body, which includes the mind, to a new body. This new body could be another human body, or the soul may be elevated to the higher, heavenly planets. A third option is that it enters the lower species, to be born again as a plant, fish, insect, bird or beast.

Hindus believe that awareness, and therefore the atman, is present in all species of life. This idea forms the basis for certain values (such as *ahimsa*, non-violence) and practices (such as vegetarianism).

The law of karma

Hindus believe that our next birth depends on our karma. Karma literally means 'action', but it also means 'the results of our actions'.

Hindus therefore talk of kind and charitable actions bringing 'good karma', and cruel acts bringing 'bad karma'. Each soul is responsible for its actions.

The soul only creates karma while in the human body. Animals have no moral choice – they act purely according to their instincts. They must wait to come into the human form before again making free choices. Those souls who go the heavenly worlds enjoy themselves, but return to earth as humans after using up their good karma.

Moksha

The cycle of birth and death is called *samsara*. It goes on indefinitely, but is not eternal. While in the human form, the soul can come to understand his or her true nature as brahman (spirit). To do this he or she must become free from all karma, and all selfish desires. The soul can then attain moksha, liberation from the cycle of repeated birth and death. Moksha is a state of *yoga*, which means 'union with God'. Yoga also refers to any process of linking with the divine.

▼ This modern painting symbolically depicts samsara, the perpetual cycle of birth and death. It is based on a verse from the Bhagavad Gita, which states, 'As the soul passes within the body from childhood to youth to old age, similarly at death the unchanging self passes into a new body'.

Dharma

Dharma is often translated as 'religion' or 'religious duty'. Dharma actually means 'duties that sustain us according to who we are'. The idea is that we have different duties according to our identity. There are two types of dharma:

1 Sanatan Dharma – the eternal relationship between the soul and God

2 Varnashrama Dharma – duties according to the body we have, involving the four varnas (classes) and the four *ashramas* (stages of life).

The system of four varnas has become what is referred to as the 'caste system' (see page 37 for more about the caste system). The four ashramas are the four stages of life as shown in the box (see also page 38).

One goal, many paths

The ultimate aim of all dharma is moksha, liberation. Although there is only one final goal, there are different ways to achieve it. There are four main paths, or yogas:

1 *Karma-yoga* – the path of selfless work

2 *Jnana-yoga* – the path of knowledge and wisdom

▲ *A colourful sadhu (holy man), who has renounced worldly comforts. For Hindus, there are four aims to human life: to become moral and righteous, to create prosperity, to enjoy worldly pleasure in an ethical way, and to get liberation from the perpetual cycle of birth and death. The last aim is most important, the final goal.*

3 *Astanga-yoga* – the path of meditation

4 *Bhakti-yoga* – the path of devotional service

Many Hindus strive to follow one or more of these paths. Most believe that members of other religious traditions also follow these paths in their own ways.

Four varnas

Shudra – craftsperson, worker
Vaishya – farmer, trader, business
Kshatriya – police, army, government
Brahmin – priest, teacher, intellectual

Four ashramas

Brahmachari Ashrama – student life
Grihastha Ashrama – householder life
Vanaprashta Ashrama – retired life
Sannyasa Ashrama – renounced life

God

Hindu people usually refer to God as 'Bhagwan' or, less often, 'Ishvara'. The Hindu teachings tell us that God can be found in three places:

1 Everywhere, as brahman, the all-pervading spirit. God is aware of everything. The soul (atman) is a part of God and is also brahman (eternal and conscious).

2 Within the heart of all living beings. God can be detected in animals as instinct, and in humans as conscience, inspiration and exceptional ability.

3 Outside – far beyond this world. God lives in the eternal, spiritual world.

The trimurti

Although God is one, he has unlimited forms and qualities. These are represented by the thousands of Hindu deities.

There are three main deities, called the *trimurti*. Brahma is the creator, Vishnu the maintainer, and Shiva the destroyer. All matter goes through three phases that correspond to these deities: creation, staying for some time, and final destruction. Some Hindus say that these deities are all equal. Others claim that one is Supreme (usually Vishnu or Shiva), while the others are subordinate and less powerful.

➤ *Shiva the destroyer. His followers, called Shaivas, usually consider Shiva to be Supreme and make up one of the three main denominations or 'strands' within Hinduism (see page 5). In this painting you can also see Brahma and Vishnu (in the top left-hand corner). At the bottom left stands Shiva's wife, Shakti or Parvati. Also shown is Ganesh, one of Shiva and Shakti's two sons, with his elephant head.*

Goddesses

Most Hindus believe God to be both male and female. The three main deities, the trimurti, each has a wife. Sarasvati, the goddess of learning and the arts, is the wife of Brahma. Lakshmi, goddess of wealth and fortune, has Vishnu as her husband. Shakti, Mother Nature, has many different forms including Parvati, Durga and Kali. She is Shiva's wife.

Worshippers of Shakti (also called Devi) make up the third main group within Hinduism (see page 5), known as Shaktas. They mainly worship Shakti (Shiva's wife), in the form of Parvati or Durga (see page 15). Many Shaktas worship other goddesses, including Sarasvati and Lakshmi who are considered to be Shakti's daughters.

▼ Goddess Sarasvati is shown here with her husband Brahma, the creator, who has four heads. Sarasvati is said to have cursed her husband and, as a result, although he is honoured by most Hindus, he is worshipped in only one place – a town called Pushkar in India.

Forms and avatars of God

In addition to the trimurti and their wives, there are many other deities, including:

- Rama and Krishna, two important *avatars* ('descents' or 'incarnations') of Vishnu.

- Hanuman, the monkey-warrior. He is physically powerful and, as Rama's devoted servant, helped Rama rescue Sita (see page 19). Hanuman is a favourite with sportspeople and soldiers, and is worshipped for help and good fortune.

- Ganesh and Skanda, sons of Shiva and Shakti. Ganesh is famous for his elephant's head and, as the remover of obstacles, is venerated before any important event. His brother, Skanda, is popular in southern India, where he is known as Murugan.

- Surya, the sun god, is often considered a form of Vishnu. Surya is especially worshipped during the festival of Pongal in southern India. There are many other gods who have responsibility for running

the universe; these include Chandra (the moon god), Agni (in charge of fire), Vayu (the wind god), Yama (the god of death and justice) and Indra (the god of rain and king of the heavens). These deities, popular in early Hinduism, are rarely worshipped these days.

➤ *Vishnu, the sustainer, with his wife Lakshmi, goddess of wealth and good fortune. Vishnu's followers are called Vaishnavas, one of the three largest Hindu denominations. They usually think of Vishnu as God, the Supreme Deity. Vishnu is famous for his avatars ('descents' or 'incarnations'), the most popular of which are Rama and Krishna (see page 19).*

The religious texts

Hindus largely base their ideas on religious texts. There are two main groups of texts called *shruti* and *smriti*. The shruti texts are considered by many Hindus to be more important, but they are philosophical and hard to understand. The smriti help to explain the shruti, often through stories.

The four Vedas

The first texts were called the *Vedas*. There are four main books including the oldest, the *Rig Veda* (see page 4). An important part of the *Vedas* are the philosophical texts called the *Upanishads*. The *Upanishads* are one of four broad categories within the *Vedas*. Although they may be interspersed within the *Vedas*, they have also been compiled as separate books.

The ideas in the *Vedas* and the *Upanishads* are further discussed in an important book called the V*edanta Sutra*, part of the smriti. 'Vedanta' means the 'conclusion of the *Vedas*'. 'Sutra' means an 'aphorism' – a saying that is short but which has deep meanings contained within it.

Main Hindu holy books

Shruti ('that which is heard')
The Vedas *(prayers and philosophy)*
The Upanishads *(philosophy)*

Smriti ('that which is remembered')
The Vedanta Sutra *(aphorisms)*
The Puranas *(stories and histories)*
The epics: (1) The Ramayana
             (2) The Mahabharata
The Bhagavad Gita *(philosophy)*

The Puranas

The *Puranas* are books of ancient stories, or myths ('Purana' means 'ancient'). Many Hindus do not consider myths to be untrue. Rather, they believe that myths describe other dimensions which are often beyond this world. Most of the *Puranas* are dedicated to Shiva (and Shakti) and to Vishnu, who appears in many forms and incarnations. Of the ten main incarnations of Vishnu, Rama and Krishna are the most important.

◄ *A gathering of people in India listen to a Hindu guru speak on a Hindu text. 'Upanishad' means 'sitting close to'. It refers to the student who would sit near the guru, the spiritual teacher. In Hinduism, the guru is still considered important to help the student understand the Vedas and the other holy books.*

➤ *This 13th-century painting from Orissa in eastern India shows a scene from the* Devi Bhagavata Purana. *The story, in which Durga kills the buffalo demon, illustrates the powerful and assertive role that women play in both social and spiritual life in Hinduism.*

There are eighteen main *Puranas*. The most famous are those describing the activities of Krishna. Krishna is celebrated for his activities as a child and youth in the village of Vrindavana. As a baby, he was extremely mischievous, stealing butter and feeding it to the monkeys. As an adult, he moved to the city of Dvaraka, and became a powerful king.

Another popular book, the *Devi Bhagavata Purana*, tells the story of the goddess Durga. She slayed a demon who took the form of a buffalo. All the gods combined could not kill the demon, but Durga easily defeated him.

The Ramayana

The *Ramayana* is one of two Hindu epics (the other being the *Mahabharata*). It means 'the journey of Rama'. It tells of how Lord Rama, an incarnation of Vishnu, was tricked into leaving his kingdom. His brother, Lakshman, and his wife, Sita, decided to go with him to the forest. While they were there, the wicked Ravana kidnapped Sita. In search of his dear wife, Rama met a race of powerful and intelligent monkeys, and their general, the monkey-warrior called Hanuman.

After long travels, Hanuman eventually found Sita, captive on the island of Lanka, Ravana's kingdom. With one huge leap, he returned to mainland India and assembled a monkey army on the southern coast. Under his direction, the troops constructed a floating bridge, marched on to Lanka and defeated Ravana's forces. Rama killed Ravana and was reunited with his wife. In jubilation, the heroes returned home to Ayodhya. It was the night of the new moon and pitch dark. As the army entered the city, the citizens lit thousands of lamps to light up the way.

Verse from the Ramayana

'If one surrenders unto me sincerely, saying "My Lord, from this day on I am fully surrendered unto You," from that time on I give that person protection. That is my vow.'

Lord Rama to Hanuman

The Mahabharata

The *Mahabharata* is the longest poem in the world. It recounts the story of the five Pandava brothers (the sons of King Pandu) and their hundred cousins, headed by Duryodhana. The eldest of the Pandavas was the rightful heir to the throne of the Indian empire. In a game of dice, he was cheated out of his empire by Duryodhana. The Pandavas spent thirteen years in exile but when they returned to claim their kingdom, Duryodhana refused to give it up. The Pandavas had no alternative but to fight. Armies from all over India assembled on the plains of Kurukshetra, just north of present-day New Delhi.

Lord Krishna had always supported the five Pandavas. Before the battle of Kurukshetra, Krishna offered the third brother, Arjuna, and his cousin, Duryodhana, a choice. Either they could have him (the Supreme Lord) on their side – but not in any fighting capacity, or they could employ the services of his army. Arjuna chose Krishna. Duryodhana scoffed at Arjuna's choice and chose Krishna's troops. Arjuna asked Krishna to be his charioteer. These events set the scene for Krishna speaking the *Bhagavad Gita*, which forms one chapter towards the end of the *Mahabharata*.

The Bhagavad Gita

As the armies made their final preparations, Arjuna asked Krishna to draw up his chariot between the two armies. He wanted to estimate the strength of the enemy. Seeing all his cousins, his grandfather and his military teacher in the opposite ranks, he broke down and said, "Krishna, I shall not fight. I am confused about my duty. Please become my teacher and instruct me."

Krishna first praised Arjuna. As a warrior, he was not only brave but also considerate. He was concerned about how his actions would affect others. But Krishna then criticized the prince for thinking that his body was his real self, and that his cousins were special because of some physical relationship. Krishna spoke the entire *Bhagavad Gita* to relieve Arjuna of this misconception, and to help him understand his eternal, spiritual nature.

Arjuna and his brothers won the battle of Kurukshetra and took charge of the vast Indian Empire. After Lord Krishna left this world, some 36 years later, the five brothers retired to the Himalayas. Krishna's departure marked the beginning of the Kali yuga, the age of hypocrisy and false-leadership.

➤ *Krishna and Arjuna on the chariot just before the Battle of Kurukshetra. After hearing Krishna's instructions, Arjuna fought with determination and after eighteen days he and his brothers emerged victorious. This Indian painting dates from the 18th century.*

3 Spiritual and religious practices

Many Hindus consider five practices essential to their spiritual well-being. These practices largely focus on developing awareness of their own spiritual nature and their relationship with the Supreme (God). The five basic practices are dharma (or living a virtuous life – see page 14), worship, festivals, pilgrimage and rites of passage.

Worship

Hindu worship involves a wide range of practices – even dance is included! The most common practice is puja, ritual worship of the murti or sacred image. Puja is central to the process of bhakti-yoga, the path of devotion (see page 14).

▼ *A murti of Krishna during temple puja.*

Types of worship

- Yoga and meditation
- Havan – *the sacred fire ceremony*
- Pravachan – *a talk or lecture on the holy books (see page 18)*
- Puja – *ritual worship of the murti (sacred image).*

Puja may include other practices, such as:

- Darshan – *'seeing' the deity*
- Prasada – *offering and receiving sacred food (see page 40)*
- Arati – *a ceremony in which a lamp is offered (see page 24)*
- Seva – *active service to the murti (such as cleaning the temple)*
- Bhajan and kirtan – *singing and chanting (see page 10)*
- Pradakshina – *circumambulation*

All these practices are not solely in veneration of the murti. For example, arati may be offered to the guru or to other holy people.

In our own words

"On my altar at home I have a photo of my spiritual teacher. I offer arati to him each morning. The guru is not God, but because he is dear to God, we offer him respect and worship. We believe that we receive the grace of God by serving and pleasing those people who are dear to him."

Sunil Sharma, 20, Washington D.C., USA

▼ *People light lamps to perform the Akasa Deep puja, the 'sky lantern' festival on the sacred River Ganges. Legend says that the Ganges water was touched by the sacred feet of Vishnu. There is also a story of how Shiva caught the river in his hair as it fell to earth from heaven.*

Focuses of worship

Although most Hindus believe in one God, there are many focuses of worship. For example, there are the many Hindu deities (see page 15), often worshipped through the murti.

Hindus also worship God as represented in other ways. They believe that anything connected to God is sacred. For this reason, they may venerate lesser deities (such as Surya, the sun god), spiritual teachers (gurus), and family elders such as parents. They consider holy the land associated with a saint or incarnation of God, and many rivers are sacred (see page 31). Even the cow may be offered worship, since she represents the mother, and is therefore special. Some Hindus venerate holy trees, such as the Tulsi (sacred basil) and the Bilva. Hindus believe that without respecting what is dear to God, including all living beings, spiritual advancement is impossible.

Puja (ritual worship)

Hindus perform puja at home and in the temple. There is no special day of the week for puja, although different days are connected with specific deities, for example Shiva is often worshipped on a Monday. However, the time of day is important. The tranquil morning hours, especially before dawn, are considered best for puja. Evening worship is also popular.

Worship is often a personal matter, and can be performed alone, in prayer and in meditation. Some traditions emphasize congregational practices, such as group singing. Worship in the temple is often quite informal, with visitors arriving and leaving throughout the public ceremonies.

Puja in the temple

The temple is considered to be the home of God, or the particular deity represented on the shrine. These sacred images, or murtis, are served just like great kings or queens. The temple priests bathe them, dress them and offer them food. Puja also involves offering auspicious items, such as pure water, perfume and flower garlands. Worship usually finishes with the offering of vegetarian food to the murti.

Puja in the home

Practically every Hindu home includes a shrine. It may simply be a shelf in the kitchen with framed pictures of deities and saints. Other families set aside an entire room, with a shrine housing small murtis. Worship in the home is usually a simplified version of the elaborate temple rituals. The women often take charge, and children learn about their tradition by being actively involved.

▼ *Puja in the home in the UK. It is usually the women of the household who take charge.*

In our own words

"When I was small I had my own shrine in the bedroom, with lots of pictures of Krishna, Rama and everyone. Hanuman was my favourite. Now I often help Mum do the arati. All of our food is offered to God. My Mum puts a little of each dish into stainless steel bowls on a tray. Then she puts the tray on the shrine and says some prayers while ringing a bell. Afterwards, we all say a prayer before eating."

Karuna, aged 12, Bristol, UK

Visiting the temple

Although most Hindus worship daily at home, they also visit a temple regularly. Upon entering, they remove their shoes out of respect and for cleanliness. They come before the shrine to take darshan ('sight') of the deity. With palms together, they say a few prayers. It is customary to offer a gift of fruits, uncooked grains or flowers, or to drop a few coins in the donation box. The priest may hand out morsels of *prasad*, sacred food offered to the deity. Visitors may then sit on the floor, appreciating the atmosphere and waiting for the arati ceremony

The arati ceremony

Many people gather for the arati. There are up to six or seven services during the day. In India, the first is usually before dawn, at around 5 or 6 o'clock. Standing in front of the shrine, the temple priest offers a lamp to the murtis. The lamp usually has five wicks. The lamp, now considered sacred, is passed around the worshippers. Each worshipper passes their palm over the flames, and then touches their fingers respectfully to the forehead. The priest also offers incense, water and a flower.

During arati, it is customary for the congregation to stand. They may join in singing or chanting, with small hand cymbals, drums and other musical instruments.

◄ *Hindu ladies wait for the arati ceremony at a temple in London, UK. In some temples, men sit on one side of the temple room, women on the other. There are usually no chairs, except for the elderly who have difficulty sitting on the floor.*

Yoga and meditation

As well as being used for worship, the temple and home shrine are also places for quiet reflection and meditation. Hindu texts stress the importance of controlling the mind. It is risky to let it wander or to obey its every desire. Yoga and meditation are ways of disciplining the body and mind. Hatha-yoga, with its postures and breathing exercises, is good for the health. However, its main purpose is to control the mind and then to see directly the soul and God, both residing in the region of the heart.

Chanting

An important form of meditation is the chanting of a *mantra*. Mantra means 'that which delivers the mind'. In other words, a mantra helps free the mind from worrying about temporary things such as money, shopping, health and so on. It helps people to think clearly. In a state of peace, one becomes happy, free from yearning, fear and lamentation.

A mantra is a short prayer, or a string of sacred syllables. It may begin with the sacred syllable 'Om'. The practice of chanting mantras quietly, or silently in the mind, is called *japa*. Mantras are also chanted loudly to music. This is called kirtan.

Mantras

Common mantras include:
"Om Namah Shivaya" ("I bow down and offer my respects to Lord Shiva").

"Hare Krishna Hare Krishna,
Krishna Krishna Hare Hare,
Hare Rama Hare Rama,
Rama Rama Hare Hare"

("Oh Krishna, Oh Rama, please engage me in your service").

The Gayatri mantra (see page 33).

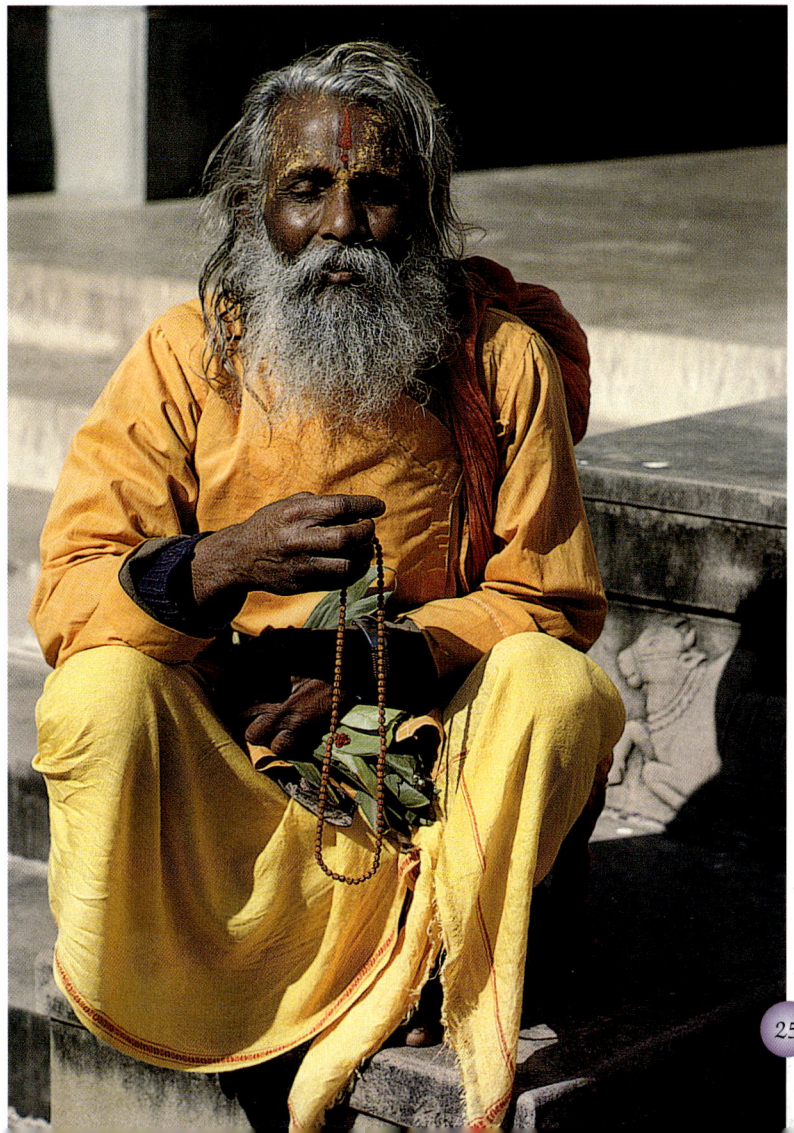

➤ *A sannyasi (see page 35) fingers prayer beads (japa-mala) during his meditation. He has taken a vow to chant almost 7,000 mantras each day, using the beads to help him count. There are usually 108 beads on each string.*

25

Festivals

In Hinduism there are hundreds of festivals every year and they vary according to region and tradition. The four main purposes of festivals are: to celebrate special events in the life of a specific deity, to mark seasonal changes and events connected to nature, to celebrate special events in the life of a holy person, and to celebrate family relationships.

Festivals of the first type are often celebrated widely throughout India and other parts of the world. Some are also public holidays. The others festivals are more likely to be celebrated in one region of India, or by people from that area. They are often connected with a specific tradition, which may follow a particular saint.

Festivals are observed by fasting and feasting, visiting temples and relatives, wearing new clothes and decorating homes and temples. There is also much music, dance and drama, as well as special acts of worship. For example, on Janmashtami (Krishna's birthday) there is a beautiful midnight arati.

Twelve important festivals

	Name of festival	Time of year	Relevant figures and significance
1	Makara Sankranti	January	*Surya: harvest festival (called Pongal in southern India)*
2	Sarasvati Puja	January/February	*Sarasvati (birthday) and beginning of spring*
3	Maha Shiva Ratri	February/March	*Shiva*
4	Holi	March	*Vishnu (man-lion avatar) and spring festival*
5	Rama Navami	March/April	*Rama (birthday)*
6	Hanuman Jayanti	April	*Hanuman (birthday)*
7	Guru Puja	July	*Sage Vyasa and one's personal guru*
8	Raksha Bandana	August	Brothers and sisters
9	Janmashtami	August/September	*Krishna (birthday)*
10	Ganesh Chaturthi	August/September	*Ganesh (birthday)*
11	Nava Ratri	Sept/October	*Shakti (Parvati, Durga and other goddesses)*
12	Diwali	Oct/November	*Lakshmi (also Rama): for some, the New Year*

The Hindu calendar

According to the Gregorian (or Western) calendar, Hindu festivals fall on different dates each year. This is because the Hindu months correspond to the actual cycles of the moon. The twelve Hindu months are shorter than the months in the Western calendar, and so a leap month (extra month) is added once every three years. There are 30 days in each Hindu month, although one day is occasionally skipped. The month is divided into two halves – the light fortnight, as the moon waxes, and the dark fortnight, as it wanes. In everyday affairs, Hindus often use Western calendars but religious observances are still worked out according to the lunar calendar.

New Year and Diwali

Hindus celebrate the New Year at different times. For many, it coincides with Diwali (the Festival of Lights). This autumn festival welcomes Lakshmi, the goddess of prosperity, into the home. It also commemorates the victorious return of Rama and Sita, as told in the *Ramayana*, and their entrance into their capital city, Ayodhya (see page 19).

▼ *Diwali celebrations in the UK. Diwali means 'row of lamps'. During the festival, Hindus decorate homes and temples inside and out with thousands of divas (lamps).*

Spring festivals

One of the first festivals in the Hindu year is dedicated to the worship of Sarasvati, the goddess of learning and the arts. On this day, Hindus welcome spring by wearing yellow clothes, and children fly brightly coloured kites. Shortly afterwards comes the biggest festival for worshippers of Shiva. It is called Maha Shiva Ratri – the great night of Shiva. Strict worshippers fast for twenty-four hours and stay up all night to attend the puja (ritual worship) of the *linga*, a stone column representing Lord Shiva.

Holi

Perhaps the most famous spring festival is Holi. It recalls the story of the saint Prahlad and the half-man, half-lion incarnation of Vishnu.

In this story, Prince Prahlad's tyrannical father was trying to kill his son. After many unsuccessful attempts, the king asked his

In our own words

"Yesterday it was Holi. We went to the temple wearing white clothes and threw coloured water all over each other. We got completely covered in it! My friends played tricks, too, like hiding from each other. We did this to remember how Krishna loved playing tricks when he was young. Then we ate long noodles, boiled with sugar and ghee."

Dhara Patel, 8 years old, UK

sister, Holika, for help. Holika had been granted a boon by the fire-god Agni which gave her special protection from fire. To help her evil brother, she carried Prahlad into the middle of a raging bonfire. However, Vishnu protected the boy and the wicked Holika burnt to ashes.

Hindus celebrate by building huge bonfires. On this day, everyone is allowed to be cheeky, even to teachers and parents! Children and adults all have fun by playing tricks, and throwing coloured powder and water over each other.

◄ Holi celebrations and fun in Pushkar, India. During Holi, Hindus hurl coloured powders and water at each other. They believe that Krishna also sported like this thousands of years ago. Krishna's birthday, called Janmashtami, falls in summer, not long after Raksha Bandana (see next page).

Nava Ratri

The longest festival, Nava Ratri, occurs in late autumn. Nava Ratri means 'nine nights', and over nine consecutive days, Hindu people meet in the evenings to worship the goddess Shakti. The favourite activities for worship are exuberant stick dances, with all the women and girls dressed in bright sarees.

Nava Ratri specifically honours Shakti, the wife of Shiva. She is often addressed as 'Devi' (goddess) and as 'Mataji' (respected mother). In Bengal, Devi is worshipped in the form of Durga, who rides on a lion and wields weapons in her ten hands.

▼ *A brother and sister in the USA celebrate the festival of Raksha Bandana. It is observed in August, mainly in the home. Women tie rakhis (protective bracelets) on the wrists of their brothers and other male relatives – even close family friends. The boys and men respond by giving gifts to their sisters.*

In our own words

"*We celebrate Raksha Bandana at home. I say a prayer asking Bhagwan (God) to protect Vijay, my brother. I then tie a* rakhi, *usually made of gold or silver tinsel, on Vijay's wrist. In return, he gives me a present and promises to look after me.*"

Dipika, aged 10, London, UK

Pilgrimage

Visiting holy places is an integral part of the Hindu way of life. Hindus undertake pilgrimage for a number of reasons: to remember and worship the divine (God, a specific deity or a particular saint), for purification and to make spiritual progress, or to perform a religious rite or ritual, such as a ceremony for a deceased person.

▼ *Bathing ghats and a shrine dedicated to Shiva on the banks of the River Ganges in Varanasi.*

Practices

When travelling, Hindus often accept voluntary hardships (austerity). These hardships can include fasting, celibacy, or travelling barefoot – also a sign of respect for sacred ground. They visit special shrines, marking the birthplace of a saint or other events associated with a story or legend. Pilgrims take darshan (sight) of the murti, receive holy food (prasad) and give in charity to the shrine, holy people and the poor. They may hear stories connected with the site, and often show respect by walking reverentially around the spot, usually in a clockwise direction.

Holy places

Most Hindu holy sites are in India and connected with a particular deity. The most famous place, Varanasi, in the northeast of India, is devoted to Lord Shiva. It is also called Benares and Kashi. Here, pilgrims scatter the ashes of their loved ones in the sacred River Ganges, believing that this helps the soul towards final liberation.

About 160 kilometres south of Delhi, the holy towns of Mathura and Vrindavan are connected to Krishna who lived there as a child and youth. On the east coast, the town of Puri is famous for its annual 'festival of the chariots', now celebrated throughout the world. In the north of the country, in the foothills of the Himalayas, there is a hilltop shrine at Vaishnoo Devi. It attracts many pilgrims, and is dedicated to the three main female deities – Lakshmi, Sarasvati and Shakti (in her fierce form as Goddess Kali).

Mountains and rivers

The Himalayas are sacred to many Hindus. In these remote peaks, and in the surrounding foothills, yogis and ascetics perform penance, doing meditation and tolerating the chilling cold. Further south, in a region that gets scorching hot in summer, lies the famous hill called Govardhana. Pilgrims offer respect by walking around it while praying. The *Puranas* tell the story of how Krishna lifted the hill to protect the local people from torrential rain sent by the rain god, Indra.

Many rivers are considered sacred by Hindus. There are seven major holy rivers of which the Ganges is most important, and bathing in them is thought to wash away one's sins (bad karma). One of the biggest events is the Kumbha Mela (bathing fair) held regularly in different towns. The *Puranas* tell the story of how the gods and their enemies, the demons, came to a truce. By churning the ocean, they produced the nectar of immortality. The nectar fell at certain spots in India, where the Kumbha Mela now takes place. Hindus believe that bathing in these places can grant moksha (liberation). In 2001, the Kumbha Mela in the town of Prayag attracted well over 20 million people!

▼ *Pilgrims bathing in the sacred River Ganges during Kumbha Mela.*

Rites of passage

For Hindus, life is an ongoing journey – a long adventure. Hindus believe that even before birth, we (the soul) have existed somewhere else. After death, we depart either to take another body or to get liberation (see page 14). This world is like a restaurant or a railway station, with people constantly arriving, meeting each other, then leaving.

For many Hindus, there are four principal stages (ashramas) throughout this one life – student life, householder life, retired life and renounced life (see page 14). There are also up to sixteen main ceremonies, which celebrate the completion of one period of life (or an entire ashrama) and moving on to the

▼ *This boy is about to have his first haircut. The priest is ringing a small bell as is customary during worship and rituals. The birth and name-giving ceremonies are the fourth and fifth samskaras. They are followed by: 6. the first outing; 7. the first grains; 8. the first haircut; 9. piercing of the ears.*

next. These rituals are called *samskaras*. They help to purify the soul so that it can be free from selfish thoughts and actions. This helps the individual move towards moksha (liberation).

Birth ceremonies

The first samskara takes place before conception. The couple prays that a good soul will enter the womb. They want the baby to grow up into a healthy person and a good citizen. During pregnancy there are two other samskaras for the healthy development of both mother and child.

At birth the *jatakarma* ceremony welcomes the baby into a new chapter of life – a new family. The father places a small amount of ghee (clarified butter) and honey on the child's tongue and whispers the name of God in child's ear. Shortly afterwards, there is a name-giving ceremony in which the infant is dressed in new clothes. At this time, it is customary for a priest to make a horoscope for the child and to predict the future.

Initiation ceremony

The next major ceremony, usually considered
the tenth or eleventh samskara, occurs
between the ages of eight and twelve. The
boy is given a sacred thread and sometimes a
new, spiritual name. He is then considered
'twice-born', a full member of his varna (see
page 37), and can begin chanting the Gayatri
mantra (see box). This samskara represents a
spiritual birth and traditionally the boy
accepts a guru (teacher).

There is a subsequent
samskara marking the actual
beginning of education, but
today the two ceremonies are
often performed together. In
previous times, boys would
go to live with their teacher
and attend the *gurukula* (the
traditional 'school of the
guru'). There they learned the
Vedas and tried to develop
good qualities, such as
honesty, cleanliness and an
attitude of service to others.

The sacred thread ceremony is
only usually performed for
boys who are members of the
three higher varnas (Vaishya,
Kshatriya and Brahmin: see
page 14). Some religious
groups perform the same ritual
for girls, but women don't
usually wear the sacred thread.

The Gayatri mantra

'*We concentrate our minds on the
most radiant light of the Sun god,
who sustains the earth, the heavens
and all that lies in between. May he
guide our intellect.*'

Rig Veda 3.62.10

➤ *A boy in India at his sacred
thread ceremony. The thread is
draped over the left shoulder and
falls diagonally across the body. After
the ceremony, the boy regularly
chants the Gayatri mantra three
times each day – at dawn, noon and
dusk. As he recites this mantra, he
will have his sacred thread wrapped
around the thumb of his right hand.*

The wedding ceremony

The wedding, the fifteenth samskara, is perhaps the most important ceremony in a Hindu's life. It marks the entrance into the household ashrama, the second stage of life (see page 14). Traditionally, parents arranged marriages, ensuring that the bride and groom shared similar tastes, interests and backgrounds. Young Hindus usually had some say in the choice of partners. Today, couples often make arrangements independently of their parents.

The actual ceremony that celebrates a wedding varies according to region and tradition. There are often several ceremonies leading up to the main event. On the day itself, various rituals symbolize union. The couple exchange flower garlands, the priest pours water over their joined hands, and their upper garments are knotted together by a woman relative.

A priest performs a havan (sacred fire-ceremony). The couple toss grains, symbolizing prosperity, into the fire and then walk round the fire together, usually four times. They then take seven steps together. Each step is to bring fulfillment of their wishes, for good food, wealth, health, children and so on. The ceremony is concluded with relatives and friends offering gifts and blessings, all followed by a grand feast.

Retirement and renounced life

Within the Hindu community, divorce is now quite widespread, especially outside India. Traditional Hinduism disapproves of it, considering marriage a firm vow and a

▼ A marriage ceremony in South India. The bride is dressed in the traditional red and gold saree and the groom wears white silk. Most ceremonies are lavish affairs, and conclude several days of ritual celebration.

lifelong commitment. However, in past times when children were grown up and settled, their parents were expected to enter the third ashrama, retired life, often spending time on pilgrimage. Today, many couples retire from work, but few formally enter the third ashrama.

Only a few men adopt the fourth ashrama, renounced life. This involves leaving home to become a sannyasi (a wandering monk) in order to prepare for death and the inevitable separation it brings. The *sannyasi* has to give up the idea that he belongs to a certain family, race, country or religion. He becomes 'a citizen of the world', trying to develop his love for God and to see all living beings equally. The renunciate also has responsibility to teach and preach, especially to householders who easily forget that all material situations are temporary. Traditionally, the ex-wife of a sannyasi stayed at home and also dedicated herself to spiritual practices.

Funeral rites

After death, Hindus usually cremate the body. They believe that this helps the soul move on to its destination. Otherwise, it may hang around as a ghost, attached to the objects of its former life.

The body is first washed and decorated with new clothes and flower garlands. The eldest son lights the funeral pyre and the priest chants prayers, wishing the soul a safe journey. Afterwards, the ashes are scattered in a holy river, such as the Ganges. This sixteenth samskara signifies the end of another chapter of life.

▼ *A body burns on a funeral pyre in Nepal, Kathmandu. The ashes will be scattered in the River Baghmati. After the funeral, relatives observe a period of mourning. This helps them come to terms with their grief and allows the departed soul to move on. There are also regular rituals performed on the anniversary of the death.*

Society, culture and lifestyle

Hinduism is not just a religion but a whole way of life. Until recently, Hindu culture was not separate from Hindu religion. Music, dance and drama all depicted religious stories and even dress and cooking were connected to spiritual practices. Similarly, the Hindu social system was based on religious ideas. One of the earliest texts, the *Rig Veda*, refers to four social classes called varnas. This developed into a more sophisticated system called 'Varnashrama dharma' (see page 14). Later texts describe the different dharmas (duties) for people, based upon how they belong to four varnas (social classes) and four ashramas (stages of life).

◄ *A traditional dance-drama in Bali, Indonesia telling the famous story of Rama and Sita. Hindu culture is rich in such tales, depicting learned saints, chivalrous kings, beautiful princesses and wicked demons. These tales often reflect the Hindu ideal of inter-dependence; that we all have different, but equally valuable, roles in society. They also teach about human virtues such as honesty, wisdom, courage, conquering evil and protecting the innocent.*

➤ *This diagram, based on a passage in the* Rig Veda, *shows how each varna is related to a part of 'the social body'. The four varnas are:* **1***. Priests and teachers* **2***. Government, army and police* **3***. Business people, traders and farmers* **4***. Craftspeople, artists and workers.*

1 Vision
Thinking
Listening
Advising

2 Protecting
Fighting
Administering

3 Nourishing
Producing

4 Supporting
Transporting

The four varnas

According to the *Bhagavad Gita*, people belong to a particular varna according to their personal qualities and the job that suits them. The four varnas are like different parts of the social body. Each part of the human body is essential, and works with others for the benefit of the whole body (see diagram). Similarly, the idea of the four varnas was to help society run smoothly. Many Hindus claim that, in this original system, people were allowed to move between varnas.

The caste system

Over the centuries, the Hindu social system changed. Some brahmins, traditionally unattached to material things, became protective of their high positions. They taught that once born into a varna, a person cannot move from it. This protected brahmin families, and their descendants, from being demoted to lower classes. It doomed those born in lower varnas to stay in lowly occupations for successive generations.

Foreigners to India used the Portuguese word 'casta' to describe this system, from which the English word 'caste' originates. However, there are not only four varnas, but also thousands of sub-groups called *jati*. A jati often describes the exact job a person does, rather like the origins of English surnames such as 'Taylor' (tailor) and 'Smith' (blacksmith). Even today, Hindus are often still expected to marry someone from the same varna and jati.

In our own words

"My father, like my mother, was born in a brahmin family, but he is a businessman. He doesn't mind if I later get married to someone outside our community. He's religious but also very open-minded. I think that the caste system is a problem in Hinduism. Perhaps the original system was okay, but I feel that more recently it has became corrupt."

Jayesh Sharma, aged 23, Leicester, UK

▲ *Mahatma Gandhi. Like him, many modern Hindus disagree with the hereditary caste system. Gandhi is also famous for teaching about ahimsa (non-violence).*

Mahatma Gandhi

Mahatma Gandhi (1869-1947) was a holy man and politician, and is probably the best-known Indian of the 20th century. He helped to negotiate Indian independence from British colonial rule, but he was bitterly disappointed by the partition of his beloved country (see page 10). He was assassinated in 1947.

Gandhi drew much of his strength and conviction from the Hindu teachings, but he objected to the hereditary caste system. By that time, some Hindus had been called 'untouchables', indicating that they were lower than even the fourth varna, the shudras. They were given only the lowest jobs, such as cleaning the streets or working with leather. They were often banned from eating with others, entering temples or drawing water from village wells. Gandhi renamed the untouchables 'the children of God', to show his idea that everyone, as the eternal soul within, is equally important.

'Gautama's disciple'

(from the Jabala Upanishad)

'A young boy approached Gautama Muni and begged to become his student. It was customary that only brahmins would be accepted for such spiritual training. Gautama therefore asked, "Who is your father?" "That I do not know," the boy replied. "So, please ask your mother." The boy's mother admitted, "My dear son, I have known many men. I do not know who is your father." The boy returned to Gautama Muni and relayed the message, "Sir, my mother also does not know who my father is." Gautama Muni concluded, "Yes, you are a brahmin. I accept you because you are thoroughly honest."'

For practical purposes, Gandhi believed in the system of four varnas, but not in the system which was determined by birth and didn't allow equal opportunity for all (see box).

The four ashramas

The Sanskrit word ashrama has been taken into English as 'ashram', meaning 'hermitage', or 'place of retreat'. However, its literal meaning in Sanskrit is 'a place to develop spiritual understanding', indicating that all four ashramas are meant for spiritual growth.

The four traditional stages of life have never been followed by all Hindus and today few Hindus strictly follow the rules of the ashramas. Nonetheless, the idea of spiritual education, followed by material enjoyment and ultimate withdrawal from society, remains an important ideal.

Family life

Although Hinduism places great value on ultimate detachment from worldly pleasure, it simultaneously stresses the importance of family stability. The building block of Hindu society is the extended family, consisting of three or four generations living together, or near to each other. Great respect was traditionally given to family elders, who would offer guidance to younger members. The centre of practically every Hindu home is the shrine, showing that one's relationship with God should be the main focus within the family.

Women in Hinduism

Traditionally, Hindu men and women took different roles. A woman's main role was as a housewife, while a man was solely responsible for earning the family's income. These roles have changed in modern society, and many Hindu women now pursue rewarding careers. Nonetheless, they often retain their traditional values, believing that by God's arrangement men and women can play complementary roles.

There are often stories in the news about how women are mistreated in India. Some families try to secure wealth illegally by abusing the ancient system of dowry (a gift of money given to the bride by her family). These crimes are largely due to greed, poverty and other social pressures, rather than religion. Hindu texts, such as the *Mahabharata*, explain that anyone who abuses women will lose all good karma, thus diminishing their health, wealth and longevity.

Caring for others

Hindu scripture teaches that a good government looks after five sections of society: women, children, animals, holy people, and the elderly. Any society can be judged by how well it protects these five types of citizen. For example, when Hindu people retire, their children usually look after them. Within the home, children are taught to respect visiting gurus and sannyasis, who help householders remember their spiritual goals. The whole purpose of the Varnashrama dharma system (see page 14) is for the strong to protect the weak, and not to exploit them.

➤ *A Hindu family in the UK enjoys a picnic. Children's welfare has been the main focus of family life. A prominent Hindu ideal is giving shelter to dependants and not abusing their trust. For this reason, and through belief in reincarnation, Hindu texts do not sanction abortion and recommend that meat-eating be given up, or at least restricted.*

Sacred food

Food is so important to Hindus that the tradition has been dubbed 'the kitchen religion'. Offering food to God is an essential item of temple puja (worship). Similarly, at home some families eat only after the meal has been offered on the family shrine. It then becomes prasad, sacred food, which, Hindus believe, purifies the body, mind and soul.

Believing the soul to be present in all species, many Hindus practice ahimsa (non-violence) and are vegetarian. Meat is now becoming popular with those living in the West, but very few eat beef, out of reverence towards the cow and bull. In India, meat is often eaten only after ritual sacrifice to the goddess Kali (a fierce form of Shakti).

Hospitality

A popular Hindu proverb states, 'the unexpected guest should be treated as well as God'. There are many stories that show the importance of offering hospitality. A Hindu should welcome a guest with at least three items – a place to sit, pleasant words and refreshments. Hindu scriptures state that even an enemy should be treated this way! It is especially important to receive holy people into the home, to offer them *seva* (service) and to inquire from them about the importance of spiritual life.

Hospitality and humility are two of the most important values of Hinduism. They are based on the core belief that everyone is a part of the divine.

▼ *Food is offered before the shrine in a temple in the UK as part of Diwali celebrations (see page 27).*

▲ *A performance of Kathakali, a blend of dance and drama from the south Indian state of Kerala. It is typified by colourful and elaborate facemasks depicting characters from Hindu scriptures, such as the* Ramayana, the Mahabharata *and the* Puranas. *This performance is in Kerala itself.*

Hindu arts

Hindu teachings are also expressed though the arts. Until recently, almost all Indian music, dance and drama had religious themes. The performing arts are often a form of worship, and the first dances were staged in temples. On festival days, stories from the epics and Puranas are still enacted on stage.

The visual arts are represented in many temples. On the walls hang posters of the many saints and deities, and traditional paintings depict religious stories. However, one of the most lasting achievements of Hindu culture is its architecture. Temples in southern Indian temples are famous for their colossal gateways, decorated with hundreds of statues of the various gods and goddesses.

41

Village life

Hinduism developed largely in a rural setting, in the Indian countryside. Gandhi believed that the key to India's wealth and happiness lay in its villages. He daily worked at a spinning wheel and opposed the mechanization of industry, preferring instead simple cottage industries. Hindu texts state that prosperity consists not of paper money, but of natural resources, such as land and animals. Nature's gifts provide the necessities of life, such as food, clothes and shelter, and luxuries such as gold, silver and jewels. Wealth comes by God's grace, not through human endeavour alone. India, however, is now beset by poverty. Many Hindus believe that it was far more prosperous before colonialization and industrialization.

The religious practices in rural India are often different from those of the towns and cities. The focus is often on local deities, and those that protect the village. The temples are generally smaller than in the cities, and there are many small outdoor shrines. Hindu texts suggest that living in the countryside helps people more easily remember God

To Hindus, the cow and bull are considered important. The cow provides milk, from which to make yoghurt, cream, butter and ghee (clarified butter, used in cooking as well as temple rituals). Dairy products are vital to those who follow a vegetarian diet. Because the cow provides milk, Hindus consider her to be 'mother' and in this sense she is sacred. She also represents mother earth. Bulls are still used for ploughing, milling and transport. Despite widespread introduction of the tractor, for many poorer Indians the bull remains an important source of energy.

▼ *Girls carry their calves in a typical Indian village near Vrindavan, the sacred town connected to Lord Krishna. Krishna himself fondly looked after cows.*

ॐ5 Hinduism in today's world

Today, an increasing number of Hindus live in sprawling cities, such as Mumbai, Kolkata, Chennai and New Delhi. Many live overseas. With increased migration and the rise of global communications, Hinduism has moved from its ancient, rural and Indian context. It is an important aspect of today's plural societies.

An Indian religion?

There are many challenges as Hindu people adapt to the rapidly changing world. Even the idea of Hinduism as a single religion, like other 'world faiths', is relatively new! Some Hindus strongly identify their religion with India, and promote forms of Hindu nationalism. They are often concerned about attempts to convert Hindus to other religions. Other thinkers emphasize that Hinduism – the Sanatan Dharma – extends beyond India. It is a spiritual path open to everyone.

Ancient or modern?

There are many tensions between ancient practices and modern values. For many Hindus, caste remains a fundamental part of their social and religious life. It is a much-debated issue. Many Hindus feel it should be thrown out altogether. Others claim that the old system of four varnas is a useful way of organizing society, provided it is based on equal opportunity. There is also debate about the role of women. Again, some prefer modern ideas of equality. Others say that there is still value in traditional ideas, such as recognizing the differences between the sexes and their roles.

▼ *A modern Hindu temple in the city of Durban, South Africa. It represents the way Hinduism is challenged by the tensions between old and new, and between living in India and outside, in a different culture. Many Hindus believe that their ideas of spiritual equality, and practices such as yoga, are just as relevant in modern South Africa as they were in ancient India.*

Towards a healthy planet

Many Hindus are actively interested in showing how their philosophy and values can be applied in modern life. Historically, India has already made significant contributions to world culture, to the arts and science. Historians say that the numeral zero originally came from India, and Hindu writings deal with astronomy, chemistry and psychology. Indian medicine is known as Ayur Veda. It stresses the importance of healthy diet, a balanced lifestyle, and herbal remedies. Today, it is becoming increasingly popular in the West, as an alternative or complementary medicine.

Hindu people are also contributing towards preserving the environment. Hindu scriptures mention the benefits of a natural life, of planting trees, protecting wildlife and avoiding pollution. The Hindu philosophy warns against greed and recommends sustainability and long-term vision as important moral principles.

▼ *School children in Northern India take part in an environmental project aiming to preserve local forests and their wildlife. Similar projects seek to protect the sacred rivers, threatened by deforestation and pollution. Many Hindus believe that traditional values, such as non-violence and sustainability, can help address these global problems.*

The world as one family

Dealing with the consequences of environmental exploitation is one of the greatest challenges of the 21st century. Another is the growing predominance of human abuse and conflict – terrorism, indiscriminate war, economic exploitation and many other forms of oppression.

Hindu teachings suggest that these conflicts are due to a wrong perception of identity – a mistaken idea of who we are. Hinduism teaches that many people wrongly believe that the body is the self, and that happiness comes solely though its gratification. Failing to see the real person within, they tend to judge others by their bodies, seeing them as black or white, male or female, young or old. They are prone to use these bodily labels to determine who is a friend or who an enemy. Some people may even judge others as good or bad simply by the religion they follow.

The Hindu motto 'Vasudaiva Kutumbakam' means 'the world is one family'. This family includes not only humans, but all other forms of life. In all living beings, the soul (atman) is present; and despite the different ways we think of God, he (and she) is the same for all of us. This is the core message of Hinduism, the Sanatan Dharma.

A prayer for the 21st century

'May there be good fortune throughout the universe, and may all envious persons be pacified. May all creatures become calm by practising bhakti-yoga, for by accepting devotional service they will think of each other's welfare. Therefore, let us all engage in the service of the one Supreme Lord!'
Bhagavat Purana, 5.18.9

▼ Hindu priests and an Anglican vicar at an interfaith event in England. Many Hindus believe that all great religious teachers have taught similar truths, with some differences in details according to the prevalent culture and the people they were teaching. Most, if not all, religious teachers have stressed the unity of humanity and of all of God's creation.

Glossary

ahimsa The Sanskrit word for 'non-violence'.

arati The most popular Hindu ceremony in which a lamp and other auspicious articles are offered to the sacred image.

Aryan According to Hindu texts, the 'noble people'. Scholars say that the Aryans are a specific race who brought core Hindu teachings to India.

ascetic A person who deliberately accepts physical hardship, usually to progress in spiritual life

ashrama A place where spiritual life is cultivated; one of the four stages in life.

atman ('self') It can mean body, mind or soul, but ultimately refers to the 'real self', the soul.

avatar A 'descent' of God or a great soul from the spiritual (eternal) world. Often translated as 'incarnation'.

Bhagwan (Bhagavan) The most commonly used Indian term for God.

bhajan ('worship') It specifically refers to a hymn or religious song.

bhakti ('devotion') Bhakti-yoga means the path of devotional service.

Brahma The creator, one of the trimurti, the three main deities.

Brahman The 'Supreme' or 'spirit', which is eternal and which pervades and supports everything.

Brahmin A member of the highest varna; a priest, teacher or intellectual.

caste system A social system based on four varnas and other sub-groups; specifically the system determined by birth rather than qualification.

darshan ('seeing') Taking audience of the deity or a holy person.

guru A spiritual teacher. A regular teacher may also be called 'guru'.

hatha-yoga A system of yoga based on physical exercises.

havan The ancient sacred fire ceremony, still practised on special occasions.

japa The practice of reciting mantras quietly or silently on prayer beads.

jati Occupational sub-groups that form part of the caste system.

karma ('action') It also means 'the results of actions'.

kirtan ('glorification') Usually refers to the musical chanting of mantras.

Lakshmi The goddess of luck and prosperity, wife of Vishnu.

linga A form of Shiva as a rounded, cylindrical stone.

mantra A prayer or a string of sacred symbols.

meditation The action of concentrating the mind and fixing it on a single point.

moksha Liberation from the perpetual cycle of repeated birth and death.

murti A sacred image or statue, worshipped in the temple or home. It represents God or a particular god or goddess.

penance Accepting physical difficulties in order to make up for something one has done wrong.

pradakshina Circumambulation (walking reverentially around), an important feature of worship.

prasada ('mercy') Usually refers to sanctified food, offered to God.

pravachan A talk or lecture on spiritual subjects.

puja Ritualistic worship, most often of the murti.

Rama An important deity, usually considered to be the seventh avatar of Vishnu.

reincarnation The process of the soul repeatedly entering one body after another.

sampradaya An unbroken line of gurus and disciples for transmitting religious knowledge.

samsara The perpetual cycle of repeated birth and death.

samskara ('impression on the mind') Refers to the various rites of passage.

Sanatan Dharma ('the eternal religion') The eternal function of the soul, to serve God; another name for Hinduism.

sannyasi A member of the fourth ashrama (stage of life).

Sanskrit An ancient Indian language.

Sarasvati The goddess in charge of learning and the arts, and wife of Brahma.

seva The Sanskrit word for 'service', a important Hindu principle and value.

Shakti A female deity, especially the wife of Shiva (Parvati or Durga).

Shiva The destroyer. One of the trimurti, the three principal deities.

shudra A member of the fourth varna; an artisan or labourer.

Sikhism The religion founded in the 16th century by Guru Nanak.

soul In Hinduism, the real, unchanging self, different from mind and body.

trimurti The three main deities, Brahma (the creator), Vishnu (the sustainer) and Shiva (the destroyer).

untouchables People considered to fall outside the four varnas.

varna A class or social group, based on peoples qualities and inclination for a particular type of work. These days usually hereditary (determined by birth).

Varnashrama Dharma The ancient Hindu social system with different duties allocated to four varnas (classes) and four ashramas (stages in life).

Veda ('knowledge') The four *Vedas* are important Hindu holy books.

Vishnu ('the sustainer') One of the trimurti, famous for his many avatars, such as Rama and Krishna.

yoga 'Union', specifically with God, or any practice aimed at such realization.

yogi (feminine: yogini) Any person who seriously performs yoga.

yuga ('age') Four main ages which rotate like the seasons.

Timeline

c.3000BCE	According to Hindu tradition, Krishna appears on earth and speaks the *Bhagavad Gita* (Song of God). The beginning of Kali yuga (age of quarrel)
c.2500BCE	Civilizations of Indus and Sarasvati valleys at height of their powers
c.1500BCE	Aryans invade India, bringing the beginnings of Hinduism
c.1500-500BCE	*Vedas* composed in the ancient language of Sanskrit
c.500BCE-500CE	Buddhism spreads throughout India. The *Puranas* and the epics (including the *Ramayana*) written
326-184BCE	Mauryan Empire unites much of India
320-550CE	Reign of the Gupta dynasty, golden age for Hindu arts
500-1000CE	Saints in South India compose many devotional poems
800	Shankara re-establishes importance of the Hindu holy books and Buddhism declines in India
c.1050	Ramanuja teaches that God is personal, living beyond this world
1200-1500	Muslims become powerful in the north, but Hindu kingdoms flourish in the south of India
1469	Birth of Guru Nanak, founder of Sikh religion
1526	Mughal Empire founded in India. Many Bhakti saints live around this period
1600s and 1700s	Many Europeans arrive in India, mainly to trade
1757	India comes under British domination, becoming part of the Empire in 1858
1828	Brahmo Samaj founded, one of many organizations seeking to reform Hinduism
1830 onwards	Many Hindus migrate to Fiji, Malaysia, Mauritius, the Caribbean, East Africa and South Africa
1869	Birth of Mahatma Gandhi, leader in the struggle for Indian independence
1897	Ramakrishna Mission established in Calcutta by Swami Vivekananda
1947	India gains independence, but loses territory to the newly-created Pakistan
1950s-1970s	Many Hindus migrate to North America (from India), to the UK (from East Africa and India) and to other countries, such as Holland and Australia
1960s	Indian thought and practices (e.g. yoga) become popular in the West, with groups such as Transcendental Meditation and the Hare Krishna Movement
1990 onwards	Hindus become socially, academically and economically well-established in the West, building many large temples

Further reading

Krishna and Hinduism by Kerena Marchant, Hodder Wayland (2002)

The Facts about Hinduism by Alison Cooper, Hodder Wayland (2004)

Vedic Stories from Ancient India by Ananta Sakti Das, Ahimsa Books (1996)

Beliefs Values and Traditions: Hinduism by Ann Lovelace and Joy White, Heinemann (1997)

Hindu Festivals Through the Year by Anita Ganeri, Franklin Watts (2003)

The Heart of Hinduism by Rasamandala Das, ISKCON Educational Services (2002)

Index